Acclaim for *How to Write a Suicide Note*

"In her raw, passionate and unflinching *How to Write a Suicide Note*, Sherry Quan Lee has committed a bold act of courage, naming ghosts and fears that can paralyze us, reminding us that sometimes we must die in order to really live, encouraging women and people of color to re-vision our lives as artists, in order to begin anew."

—Shay Youngblood,
author of *Soul Kiss* and *Black Girl in Paris*

"Sherry Quan Lee negotiates the difficult path of language between raw and educated, bare and poetic, to bring forth searing writing that is its own truth. Even if we don't intentionally lie in our own work, *How to Write a Suicide Note* pushes us to reconsider a more honest way of speaking. It reminds us that writing is no less than an act of truth, although it holds our shame, our desire to cover, and that at every moment, with every word, we make a choice to go to truth if we are invested in our own lives."

—Anya Achtenberg,
author of *The Stone of Language, The Stories of Devil-Girl,* and creator of the *Writing for Social Change: Re-Dream a Just World Workshops*

"I love the female aspects, the sex, and the strong voice Sherry Quan Lee uses to share her private life in *How to Write a Suicide Note*. I love the wit, the tongue-in-cheek, the trippiness of it all. I love the metaphors, especially the lover and suicide ones. I love the free-associations, the 'raving, ravenous, relentless' back and forth. Quan Lee breaks the rules and finds her genius. This is a passionate, risk-taking, outrageous, life-affirming book and love letter."

—Sharon Doubiago,
author of *Body and Soul, Hard Country;* and other works

"How to Write a Suicide Note is a haunting portrait of the daughter of a Black mother and a Chinese father. It vividly captures, with powerful emotion and detail, the trials of one colorful woman's life. This book is a gem.

As a clinical psychologist, I work mostly with Native Americans, African Americans, and Latino populations, where the impact of historical trauma is apparent in their day-to-day lives. But psychoanalysis, or any directive therapy couched in white privilege, is not what is needed. Sherry's work is a perfect example of how women of color find healing: salvation is within.

Sherry dares to be who she isn't supposed to be, feel what she isn't supposed to feel, and destroys racial and gender myths as she integrates her bi-racial identity into all that she is. Her story relies on a contextual view that feminist women of color insist on—the intersectionality of race, class, age, gender, and sexuality.

Through her raw honesty and vulnerability, Sherry captures a range of emotions most people are afraid to confront, or even share. It is my pleasure to read her intimate and heartening story, but more importantly her work is a gift to the mental health community."

—Beth Kyong Lo, M.A., Psychotherapist

"Sherry Quan Lee offers us, in *How to Write a Suicide Note*, a deep breathing meditation on how love is under continuous revision. And like all the best Blues singers, Quan Lee voices the lowdown, dirty paces that living puts us through, but without regret or surrender."

—Wesley Brown,
author of *Darktown Strutters*, *Tragic Magic*, and other works

HOW TO WRITE A SUICIDE NOTE

*serial essays
that saved a
woman's life*

Sherry Quan Lee

Book #2 in the Reflections of America Series

Library of Congress Cataloging-in-Publication Data

Lee, Sherry, 1948-
  How to Write a Suicide Note : serial essays that saved a woman's life / Sherry Quan Lee.
     p. cm.
  ISBN-13: 978-1-932690-63-7 (trade paper : alk. paper)
  ISBN-10: 1-932690-63-8 (trade paper : alk. paper)
  1. Racially mixed women—Poetry. 2. Identity (Psychology)—Poetry. 3. Racially mixed people—Poetry. I. Title.
  PS3562.E3644H68 2008
  811'.54—dc22
                    2008014038

Published by: Modern History Press, an imprint of

Loving Healing Press
5145 Pontiac Trail
Ann Arbor, MI 48105
USA
http://www.LovingHealing.com or
info@LovingHealing.com
Fax +1 734 663 6861

Modern History Press

Reflections of America Series

The Stories of Devil-Girl by Anya Achtenberg

How to Write a Suicide Note: serial essays that saved a woman's life
by Sherry Quan Lee

Chinese Blackbird by Sherry Quan Lee

"The *Reflections of America* Series highlights autobiography, fiction, and poetry which express the quest to discover one's context within modern society."

From Modern History Press

To Stacy Lee Quan because she knows and understands.

To loved ones, mine and yours, whose heartache was too much for this life.

To us who find ways to live with heartache.

To writers that break open hearts and fill them with life-saving stories.

Contents

Suicide hotlines:

1-800-SUICIDE / 1-800-784-2433
1-800-273-TALK / 1-800-273-8255
1-800-799-4TTY (4889) Deaf Hotline

Acknowledgements

Thanks to Sharon Doubiago, my Split Rock Arts Program Online Mentoring for Writers mentor, for her generosity of time and expertise. Thanks to Shay Youngblood for reading *How to Write a Suicide Note* and insisting that I find a publisher. Thanks to Wesley Brown for asking why I didn't ask. Thanks to Eden Torres for giving me permission to be angry and to love. Thanks to Linda Hogan for teaching at the University of Minnesota in 1985. Thanks to my writing group, *Girls Night Out,* for listening to and commenting on much of this work (and my love life, or lack of) over the past six years; especially to Sandee Newbauer who suggested *How to Write a Suicide Note* as a title. Thanks to Lori Young-Williams who collaborated with me to write and present *Chinese Black White Women Got the Beat* — where excerpts from *How to Write a Suicide Note* first got their debut. Thanks to my neighbor, friend, and sister writer, Anya Achtenberg, for her love, her encouragement — and always having chocolate. Thanks to Kurt Seaberg whose lithograph, *Temple Guardians,* embraces both the light and the dark of my story. Thanks to Beth Kyong Lo for her clinical understanding of how poetry can save lives. Thanks to Charissa Uemura for her ability to photograph me *beautiful.* Thanks to the man and his dog for, more often than not, welcoming me to the Café and Laundry in the Woods, a quiet and lovely twelve acres of pine and spruce trees, deer, rabbits, great horned owls, cardinals, crows, and occasionally a garter snake, where I had no responsibility except to write this memoir. And, much thanks and appreciation to Victor Volkman, publisher, who responded to my query letter within an hour saying, "I believe you have an important message and one that deserves to be heard so I will do whatever it takes to see it in print" — this, even though he has never published poetry.

Introduction

It has taken me six years to complete *How to Write a Suicide Note: serial essays that saved a woman's life*. It is memoir, a writer's guide, and a guide to living.

It has taken me six years to write because I don't follow any how-to-write rules, I follow my heart, my head, and my gut; I follow my emotional and intellectual needs. I don't write every day, nor do I want to. *I want to live.*

I write to live. Attempts at suicide for me were desperate attempts to be seen, to be heard, to be loved—to be alive. *Writing saved me.*

Saved me and continues to lead me toward love. *How to Write a Suicide Note* is about writing through and beyond historical trauma and my everyday remembrances of it. It is about discovering where trauma originates, why it has subjugated me, and how I am letting it go. It is about acknowledgement of the trauma, about anger, about grieving, about saying goodbye—about endings, and, most importantly, about beginnings.

How to Write a Suicide Note started out as a leap into prose, but I only produced notes—not chapters, not even vignettes. Writing prose was uncomfortable. I thought I didn't have the vocabulary to write densely, or the time to write immensely. My friend said that my notes were poetic, why not transform them into poetry? What materialized were poems that mimic who I am—*A Little Mixed Up*, but not crazy.

For me, a Chinese/Black woman who grew up passing for White, who grew up poor, who loves women but has always married White men, writing has saved my life. It has allowed me to name the racist, sexist, classist experiences that kept me *lowdown*—that screamed at me that I was no good, and would never be any good—and that no one could love me.

Writing has given me the creative power to name the experiences that dictated who I was, even before I was born, and write notes to them, suicide notes.

I believe writing saves lives; writing has saved my life.

Sherry Quan Lee

The Dying is Almost Over

Suicide Note Number One

Dear *Self-Esteem,*

Today I am writing to destroy the lack of you. Today I am going to dress you in fine recycled clothes. I am going to wear you, the royal purple of who you are. I am going to take you out in the middle of winter and promenade you. I am going to stand you on your head and turn you inside out knowing the snow angel in the front of my house is real, her halo is my halo and every speckle of grit that garnishes our diamond textured garment is invisible glue that has sewn us together.

I know what it is to be invisible. There are people who can't see me, people who don't want to see me, people who see only the parts of me they choose to see—my tiny butt, my skinny legs, my tawny complexion.

I don't know why I am so self-effacing. I don't know why I recognize ugly, stupid, and inarticulate.

How do I write away this woman who believes God is God and I must be beautiful for him? Why do I scrub my face, then cover it in liquid rhinestones? Why do I paint my silver hair red, like hell has no fury? Why do I say, *no I'm not,* when someone says *you're pretty?*

Why do I hide my words in stuffy rooms—afraid someone will say *why are you so angry?*

Why do I play the role of martyr? I know that martyrs have no choice but to die.

I will not get rid of her. I will not write away her experience. I will not deny her existence. But I will sever her sadness and wash the blood from her knife.

The angel in the snow has no shadow. There is no outlying grief.
I see the angel herself rising. Slowly. Each proclamation, elation.
Perhaps you will see her flying.

I am trying to write this suicide note, trying to kill off my lack
of self-esteem. I am trying to make sense of why I dislike myself.

It is not a letter that can be written by one author. There are others
that must give their approval

there is the mother, and the father. There are husbands and girl friends.
There are hair stylists. There are ministers and there are professors.
There are missionaries. There are governors and presidents. There are
rapists. There are rich people. There are father-in-laws. There are brother-
in laws. There are characters in books

I am a character in a book that will save me. I will teach me how
to write and how to live. I am the angel that has always been on
my shoulder. There are others. We are writing beginnings for
endings. We are sharing our stories; we are rewriting the world.

Next to the last note
it's not about the man and the dog

though they both keep barking. It's not about good writing or bad,
the woods or the inner city.

I can write notes forever, and might have to
to live. It's okay. It's okay.

It's also okay to not write. To not write notes. To not write
suicide notes.

It's okay to put away the putting away.
The putting away of concrete things.
The putting away of judgment, of being judged.

Imagine

wherever we are, whoever we are, we are remembered.

The color red may be remembered, but not the dress or socks.
The red that is you will be remembered. Is remembered

not the poem that you wrote (maybe the poem), but its aroma,
its taste, its texture, its sound.

The writing is not good or bad. The man and the dog
are not good or bad. The woman, the husband, the sister,
the brother-in-law, the teacher, the minister are who they are.

I used to believe in purgatory, always
attempting to escape,
and getting nowhere
the paradigm is magic.

Life with a sorcerer's hand—the witch and the writer.
Allusions. Illusions.
I can make my fake self disappear

the invisible seen, the silent heard, the fearful unafraid;
angels triumphant!
Living is hard. Writing is hard. The dark clouds invite us to rest,
to mourn, to gather our black hats and swords.

I'm not who you think I am; you are not who you say you are.

It's all in the shuffling, it's how the cards are dealt. It's who
is holding the cards.

Now you see me, now you don't.
I am not today who I was yesterday.

I cannot write today what I could have written yesterday
and tomorrow ghosts will appear and angels. Slight of hand

missing the movement, the moment, the transition, the process
conjured by one's private muses.

There are no rules. There are only familiar recipes that haunt us,
speak to us, that call our name—demanding that we stir the pot
and boil the soup.

The man and the dog disappear. Abruptly.
The sun sets in the west. Evergreens lose their sharp needles.

I practice magic.

A word here, a sentence there, a poem, a story.

Abracadabra.

Mix snakes and rabbits and choke-cherry trees.
Mix black eyed peas and string bean chop suey.
Mix tuna noodle casserole and apple pie.
Mix and stir, shake and shout, and turn myself about

freedom. F R E E D O M each letter a note in the song,
in the singing, in the longing, in the giving, in the receiving.
Last line, end of the line, end of the poem, the story, the book

sets us free

they are my words and how I write them. My ghosts and my angels
and how and if and when and why I receive them.
It is my madness and my happiness and how I perceive them.
It is what I want to give and who I want to give it to.

Stir the pot or let it simmer.
Jump in or taste what's cooking.
Smell the dream and toss the nightmare.

Truth is smooth like jazz, hot like Tabasco, wet like whiskey,
salty like pork, sassy like laughter, smart like girl friends,
slick like water.

I want it to not hurt.

I want it to not waste my time.
I want it to be nobody's fault (it is).
I want it to not be fatal.

I want it to not be fatal.

I want it to sing. I want it to laugh. I want it to dance. I want
it to embrace. I want it to soar. I want it to live. I want it to live.
I want it to live. To live. I want it.

The man and the dog. I want them to live (just not with me).
I want the woman to live (just not with me).
I want the child to live (just not with me).
I want to live.
I want to live.
I want. To

write. Fewer
suicide notes.
Fewer notes.
I want to write love.
I want to write love letters.

This is a letter of love.

Last Note

Some days I awaken fueled with anxiety: *I want to shop, to eat,*
to go on vacation, to have money, to be loved, to be known.

I gather my notes, notes that will eventually save me—rough drafts
that have captured my fear, my frustration, my life. Difficult.
Painful. My fingers stiff.

My head aches; my heart aches. I keep writing. Overwhelmed.
Exhausted. The dying almost finished; the book almost written.

Understanding waits for the end that is the beginning; this
is how life is.

Intellect grinding raw the imagination, details of any day, tedious.

Why do I do this? Procrastinate. Alarms blast me from beds
that have dirtied me and I must scrub clean uncertainty.
Dress in morning blush and hush nightmares.

Drive and eat and shop and gamble until lucky sevens shake loose
the losing and the words come tumbling. Jackpot.

Yes, by then, I've lost some of the verse, the lines jagged, the love
lost, pummeled to past tense soon to be ignored. Unlike
the cold winter.

I smoke wearing fleece gloves. Smoke hangs in the air like
frigid poems burning holes in hands that need to write

suicide notes, suddenly

after weeks, or even months of rumination history remembers
near death, but never buried: *cut, slashed, drowned, disappeared,*

masqueraded. Extermination of one button of my soul or another

words whistling to be heard, sour notes.

I borrow someone's dog to walk. I talk to my sister. I list
the books I want to read, the movies I want to see. I cook,
I eat, I sleep while

the writer resists the writing, the poet resists the prose, the woman
resists the man, the child resists the mother, the city resists
the country, youth resists old age, survival resists suicide; and, then

I write. Endings stringing along until they are knots
that can't be untied; gnarled and tight, flight impossible.

Blue spruce tangled in intricate webs of spiders' and angels' wings.

Sex reeks of love, yet semen are sophisticated enough to know
the difference between coming and going; and, again

I write. Notes that I will revise. Notes that will reinvent themselves.
Notes that will sting and notes that will sing—my mouth open,
unbridled; words rippling

from an underground choir, having waited ever so anxiously
to be heard.

This is the first suicide note I have written since I was twenty.
An elegy not clamoring for anyone's attention. I don't give it
to the boyfriend, the dead father, the woman, the man, the mother,
the son, the siblings, the minister, the teacher, the therapist.

I read it again, and again, and again until it makes sense, until I say

no to the poppies, the swallowed spit, the burning, the hanging,
the gun

until I acknowledge the lovers and the love, until I don't need
to get out of your bed reaching for a pen and paper, until I can
remember in the morning what didn't need to be written
in the middle of the night, until I can say

I am still here, I am here, I am here.

Death Wears Black

"When artists render up the truth of their lives and those of others, it is as if they are cartographers introducing us to foreign worlds. Even with that, the world of pain is a place unreadable by many. Sometimes it is the pain of the earth, not of any one individual." —Linda Hogan

Suicide is her companion. Not a shadow; but
an itch beneath her skin. Sometimes it surfaces, blue
welts and protruding life lines. Death in masquerade,
wears black, collects memory—slowly. Life wears

red, is always teasing, "I love you."

Suicide is the answer.

I am who I am not.
I am not, who you say I am.
Who you say I am is who you want me to be.
I am who I am becoming.
I never was.
Until now. Death

invites life.

She is not the wife, not the mother, not the partner, not the friend.
She is not White. She is not Black. She is not Asian. She is not
        an immigrant (neither was she born here).
She is not smart.
She is not young.
She is not beautiful.
Everyone says she is angry,

        and I am.

Listen to the earth, the wind, the rain, the raven. Listen.

Suicide is her mantra, a familiar song to cut the pain.

She started singing when she was nineteen.

Was I murdered or did I kill myself?

One or the other was going to relieve her madness,
she was sure of it.

Break the mirror, break the mirror, break the mirror.

Listen to the earth, the wind, the rain, the raven. Listen.

She tried to hang on to the only man in her life, God the Father.
He was as much a figment of her imagination as any man.

"Dear God, the only father I know, love me."

Or, maybe she started praying the prayer when she was five,
the year her father disappeared.

Maybe she is still praying!

How do you know if someone is important if he doesn't exist?

How do you know if you are important if you've never existed?

Last year, I tried to commit suicide three times. I lie.
The third time I wasn't thinking about killing myself.
I was only thinking about swallowing my sorrow with loud music.

She is dwelling in death so deep she can't wake up in the morning.
She can't sleep at night. She doesn't want

to be alone.

The music was so loud my VW Beatle rocked, back and forth,
back and forth like the first time I said no.

The one thing she knew wouldn't save her were the pills.
She was still smoking (and drinking) and she was as crazy
as she remembered she used to be.

                                        Beware of what you swallow.

I was inside a three-car garage, my white car running.

A man and a dog smelled gas; they didn't want to die.

She is saved by love and suicide notes. One and the same.

A new beginning.

Listen to the earth, the wind, the rain, the raven. Listen.

Because Writing Saves Lives

Rhetoric. I don't know what the word means
or how to use it in a sentence.

Pay attention to audience, purpose, exigency—
the rhetorical situation.

Who is my audience? You.
What is my purpose? To save lives.
Why? Because I want to live, I want you to live.
Because I am a writer and I want you to be a writer.

Because writing saves lives.

Writers I admire break my heart because they have heartbreaking
stories to tell and they tell them because they know there are others
like me who want to hear them because our lives have been broken
and we have stories that break hearts and broken hearts
are open hearts and anything open can be filled
with knowledge and possibility and full hearts must empty
so stories are always coming and going

> *clutch every story, every word, every syllable of want, of need, of lust,*
> *of passion, of chaos, of gratitude, of tears, of laughter, of choice,*
>
> *of necessity,*
>
> *of whisky, of wine,*
>
> *of culture, of song,*
>
> *of knives, of fingernails, of whispers, of lies, of screaming, of prayer,*
> *of touching/*
>
> *of not wanting to be touched,*

of sickness, of silence, of tenderness, of motherhood,

of hearts attacking,

of suspicion,

of country western, of the blues, of rejection, of aha's and hallelujah's,
of cayenne pepper, and wasabi, of sleepless nights,

of unemployment, of bankruptcy, of bruises, of fear, of frantic,
of homelessness,

of blessings, of jackpots, of risk, of risqué, of flirting, of red shoes,
of fantasy,

of crazy,

of knowing/of not knowing

When you can, write.
When you can't live.
When you can't live, write.

I am no longer shamed by who you say I am or what you say
I don't know. I know how to break a few hearts.

I can teach you.

It's about context. I can answer your questions with my life.

How to Revise a Rough Draft

It's time to stop writing suicide notes.
Time to stop saying goodbye.
Time to say *the end*

and begin

to revive

ego has been waiting, willfully, since birth to live.
Not to be not buried in the womb, or glow outside the body,
but to beat inside the heart, my heart,
regularly, rhythmically, confidently.

It is time to stop running.
Stop killing the messenger.

      I am not the messenger.
      (Why did I ever think I was?)

I was the mother of grief, the crying woman
      the listener
            the comforter
                 the healer;

no, that is someone else's story.

I was the judge, the jury, the prison guard. Righteous;
I threw love out with each new lover

ran from my own convictions/and theirs. Marathon
junkie, I ran! Saving myself from my self-

hatred.

Hallelujah. Glory! Glory! Hallelujah!

I could have been buried in someone else's story.
Lived someone else's life.
Dummied down, never looked up.

The blue spruce were locked on one man's island.
Each glaring tree needled with dark secrets.
His and mine.
> *I love you; I need you*
> *I don't love you; I need you.*

Here, take mine. And he did.

And, I let him

last in a series of life-long serial saviors

> *loneliness would have killed me deader than abuse*

I can count them. Women and men and houses and jobs
and friends.

See them disappear.

I spew them out like Devil Woman. Mad Woman. Mean Woman.

How to separate the evil from the good.
How to separate the need from the love.
How to know the men from the women.
How to know the end from the start.

How to revise a rough draft and make your life better.

Scatter the Trash

Suicide Note Number Two

Dear Father-in-Law,

This is my last will and testimony. I am killing the white girl.
I leave to you the Polynesian girl, the one your son claims
that I am. (I am not from Polynesia. My father is from China.
My mother is Negro. Would you like to see my birth certificate?)

I assume, considering your son's fear, the color black
is distasteful to you. I myself wear it well, but not often.
It makes other people uncomfortable, including my Black mother.

Truth is a legacy I will leave to my children, your grandchildren.
They will not live with the lie I've lived with all of my life.
What they do with the truth is up to them. I will honor
who they are.

(Choice is only an option if you know what your options are.)

It will be difficult for my sons, your grandsons, but not as difficult
as it has been for me living with secrets. They will have a mother
who knows and acknowledges they are beautiful, and smart.
A mother who knows they are afraid. A mother who is afraid
for them.

Your son pleads, "my parents like you, why tell them you are Black
and have them not like you?"

My response, "because I don't like my masqueraded self.
I don't like my silence. I don't like lying under white sheets.
I don't like any man loving me for who I am not,
for who they want me to be. I do not like being afraid.
I do not like powdering my face, straightening my hair.
How many times will I be asked by people who see me

with my brown babies, *is your husband Black?"*

No, but I will wish he was.

I have no visibility and that makes me sad.
Black people recognize me, though, and Asians.
You, like many white men, say "but you're different."

"Yes, I am."

My dreams were the same dreams as other high school girls.
Love, marriage, children, a house in the suburbs, a two car garage.

Your wealth helped me achieve my dreams. But I am not happy.
My dreams are nightmares.

Your son went to college, he doesn't have the student loans I will
someday acquire. (All students of color don't receive scholarships.)
What did he learn? How many empty bottles of booze it takes
to fill the basement of a rented house? His wealth dangling
from a family tree.

With your money we purchased a rambler with a white picket fence.
I appreciate your generosity. But, I'm tired of fences.
Will your generosity continue when I kill the white girl?

I have no regrets, death is life.

Nevertheless, your grandchildren will love and respect you.
They will embrace their Bohemian/German grandparents
as well as their Black/Chinese grandparents, although intimacy
will never be possible.

They will worry about their lonely mother, accepting her and not as she searches for love

but they will not ache for her the way she aches

and, they will not understand why they themselves sometimes ache

my sons will not die young or by their own will;
I will die for them and hope it makes a difference

        martyrs are heroes only after they die.

Hereby, I leave my words in what is now a public void,
cram white space with black ink, purge invisibility and silence
with incantations.

There will be more in-laws, more beginnings and endings—
great-grandsons who may or may not wish to know who they are.

With no regrets,

It's about money

when you have the time you don't have the money
when you have the money you don't have the time.

Most of the time I don't have the money

but, I've had access to money
the last husband, the first girlfriend

I am not lazy.

Gypsy woman: I ran, I searched, I believed
happiness was a door I could open,
that love was someplace I hadn't yet been

there were roadblocks

there were *marriages and children and education,*
there was dancing and drinking and shopping and sex

don't settle for less, don't settle. I never did. Perhaps
I should have.

You can't manage money you don't have

I was taught this in college

I didn't think it was about being poor, I thought
it was about being stupid.

The divorce settlement was fair: a condo, a used car,
and a retirement portfolio.

Within three years it was gone,
money spent like the girlfriend I was trying to impress

washers and dryers
stoves and refrigerators
another bed

paint and sheetrock

a new bathroom
a new roof

wastebaskets

towels and sheets

desks

patios and decks

Japanese Maple trees

tennis shoes and sweat pants

airline tickets

casinos

restaurants
entertainment/entertaining
margaritas and red wine

gifts

dry cleaning

dog food
dog grooming

locks and keys

it wasn't her fault. She didn't know I was spending
my future. She wanted to give me everything—she did,
but it wasn't enough. I wanted to give her everything too.

Filing bankruptcy didn't make me a free woman

some things still had to be paid: student loans
and taxes and guilt and remorse. I work three jobs but,

I'm always broke and broken. I've got a low credit line
credit card that is always maxed, and a loan for an antique bed
which was a spur of the moment need to honor sleeping
alone again

sure, I'd like to spend to improve the economy, but spending
takes money. Can the President live on $30,000 a year
and still shop, still golf? How soon would his credit
and personality run out?

I am most distressed, most depressed, most suicidal
when I don't have money

(or a lover).

A girlfriend asked, "How much?"
How much *insurance* would it take to keep you?
Apparently not enough

insurance might have been a Freudian slip.
I'm sure it was *assurance* that I desired.

So You Want Me to Write About
My Chinese Father

Asians are in, you say, write about your father

Did I tell you he was short?

I am angry. This is a good time to write.

Kung Fu, lucky bamboo, Chinese calligraphy

Asians sell books, you say, write about your father

prosperity, good fortune, happiness and health

When you are angry, keep writing.

East meets West

My father left China when his father died,
left his mother, brother and sister never
to see them again

I am not angry with my father

an immigrant, father was nine, a kid fending for himself
selling vegetables off the back of a flat bed truck

Your father is exotic you say, write about your father

mandarin collars and take out food box purses
made in China, mail order brides, girl babies

My father left me when I was five

he was supposed to marry a Chinese bride,
but he gave up all things Asian

fed us chow mein
stopped speaking Chinese, prayed Catholic

Your father is Chinese, you say, write about your father

Father liked to gamble bet black babies and a wife
for a whiter kind of life.

I have much to say about my father.

Father went to college. Mother had an eighth grade education.

I don't want to hear about your Black mother, you say, tell me
about your Chinese father

Mother was born here, slavery not a choice.
Living in America has different meanings for different people.
Father was proud. Mother ashamed. Neighbors had shot guns.

I have more to say about my father.

_____

Stop. Read what you have written. Stop.

Play rock and roll music. Dance. Shower.

There are no photos of my father and me together.

Dress as if you had someplace to go, something to do,

someone to be with who understands.

Wear something sexy. Something quirky. Something thematic.
High heels or steel toed boots. Something that will make men
pay attention.

Walk out the door, get in your car. Have fun. Buy flowers.
Be beautiful.

Don't think about your father or the man in the woods
who is sleeping.

Later, there will be time to revise.

Scatter the Trash

Let's see if we can scatter the trash

move it from South Scandinavian Minneapolis.
Move it quickly. Move it
before the day I was born, January, '48

even before I was born was too late. Already
I had three older sisters —

let's scatter the trash quickly
before the boy is born — the son, the brother

too late

let's see if we can scatter the trash
before the Chinese father disappears
before he escapes to a more acceptable
American life, where the wife has red hair and ivory skin,
a wife that doesn't need
to cover black lies, a mother who doesn't need
to deceive her children — *you are not Negro.*

What if the white trash that I was had been scattered
before I was born?

My sons, who are now 28 and 25, would have less garbage
to get rid of.

I keep a clean house where truth reigns, though truth
has its own stench. It's recognizable. It's antiseptic.
It's seductive. It seeps into thin lives in believable increments.
My sons have white, apple pie, middle-class, look-at-me fathers

do they suffer loss of memory or imagination
their garbage sweet smelling, empty
of other people's prejudices and incriminations

racism, after discrimination was supposed to have ended

have any of my relationships been about love?

My grandchildren will probably agree
with my Black mother,

don't tell anyone that you are.

They will probably agree with my Chinese father,

enlist, fight to uphold someone else's dignity.

My roommate is compulsive about recycling—
paper, plastic, tin cans.

It's useless, I say feeling guilty.

Recycling means the garbage never goes away,

this is a tricky analogy.

The garbage was here the day I was born. 55 years later,
it's still here, no matter how much I try to scatter it.

My friend says he has a well, doesn't have to worry
about conserving water. I say, it's my responsibility
as a writer, to be concerned about more than my own well.

Yet, I'm still holding on

to every piece of garbage, every word, every action
that pretends I don't exist, or if I do,

I'm worth less than garbage.

Quan, Lee Quan, Quan Lee. Maybe I should just name myself
trash—live with it,

stop writing,

erase my future.

He's Just My First Husband

1.

"I don't know how to love him, he's a man, just a man,"
Mary sang to Jesus in the rock production of Jesus Christ Superstar.

2.

She bought the blue bicycle
with panniers, a kickstand, and a solid lock

transportation to freedom after divorce number four

menopause wasn't a factor.

3.

Nurses pumped my stomach. The doctor arrived in his white coat
and white sensibility, asked "are you going to do it again?"

4.

You were the wrong height.
The wrong white.
The wrong sentimentality.
A virgin.

5.
                    valium and anti-depressants

6.

She was fifty-two years old and hadn't ridden a bicycle
since she was ten when she crashed
into a fire hydrant and bled for the first time.

7.

Lie #1:	He loves her.
Lie #2:	He knows what she needs.
Lie #3:	He's not married.
Lie #4:	She's his only lover.
Lie #5:	He's not jealous and controlling.
Lie #6:	She's not drinking.
Lie #7:	He's not sleeping in his wife's bedroom.
Lie #8:	She loves him.

8.

I rode it to the grocery store.
I bought copper salmon and garlic filled olives.
I stopped at the liquor store.
I bought two bottles of *Jest Red*.
Panniers full, I rode down black topped streets, pedaling hard
up big hills, pedaling lightly on flat ground, coasting
down small hills. It was only three miles to the party, but
it was a long ride.

9.

Suicide notes are self-inflicted. She wrote this one in college.
She is not your daughter, your girlfriend, or your wife.

10.

Each time I ran away from an ex-lover, her arms were open.
She comforted me with sarcasm and wit. We binged on wine
and cigarettes.

11.

I left husband number one in Boston to seek therapy in Minneapolis
because he said I was crazy; he continued to drink and get drunk,
and married a woman in California who had a father.

12.

She hadn't known there were bikes, designed by a woman
to fit a woman — to make women happy, cycling.

13.

He said, if someone sues you for telling the truth
it's bound to make your writing more profitable.

14.

He's just my first husband, there will be more.

15.
                    she's getting better but it will take a long time

16.

Christmas Eve I celebrated another homecoming in a bar
and slept in a downtown hotel with another drunk. Christmas Day
I got a gift from my girlfriend's father while her mother
wasn't looking.

17.

Are you crying because you're afraid you'll get pregnant?
Don't worry. I've had a vasectomy.

18.

No one expected her. No one recognized her.
Who is that riding the blue bicycle?
Who is that in the red tank top and black riding shorts?

19.

I can't wait any longer for the drugs to make me sane
or for the minister to leave his wife.

20.

The first boy she dated married a girl from Japan. The second boy
she dated married a woman from Brazil. The third boy she dated
married his cousin.

21.

She is discharged before her family or friends will know
she is crazy. Before they will know she is dead.
Before they will arrive at the hospital and take pity on her.
Before any one will react

abracadabra

and make her visible

22.

We married for the wrong reasons: you for love, me
for the possibility.

You followed me everywhere;
I didn't like the way you walked or the length of your fingers.

One day you were lost and disappeared.

23.

Each time he called her his China Doll. Each time he said, *but
you're different*. Each time she was the only Black/Chinese woman
at his office parties—the only colorful person. Each time he got up
and washed off his semen after they made love. Each time
she got drunk so she could make love. Each Sunday they entered
the suburban Christian Church, congregation white.

24.

She didn't know me.
Her reach too short,
counting rosary beads
and Ten Commandments

remnants of fear and desire in her house

25.

your lightness, your darkness
weighed me down. Pummeled me
with your demands and indecision

my first anxiety attack

whatever I said it was wrong.

26.

The minister says, you're ruining my career, the boyfriend says
stay out of my girlfriend's life, the ex-husband says
your therapy isn't working.

27.

I don't know how long it will be before I am dead
and able to start living.

28.

There is no space for me to say anything
even if I knew what I wanted to say

I write a few poems.

29.

Beauty surrounded her. Fresh flowers in a small vase.

I did whatever you wanted me to do,
went wherever you wanted me to go
ate whatever you wanted me to eat.

30.

Eventually he disappears leaving the
I'm sorry I didn't mean to hurt you note.
inside a book by Rod McKuen.

31.

The woman I loved, I loved because she reminded me of you.

32.

She had been sitting on one hard provincial chair or another from the time she turned eighteen. Mother protected her, wouldn't let her go near the water, wouldn't let her drown.

33.

Not knowing how to let her love me
without her knowing that a kiss
isn't always just a kiss

how often were we drunk?

34.

No one will miss me. And no one could find me if they did.

35.

What is the price of desire?

36.

Your therapist asked if you were a lesbian, you said
no, but I know

37.

you loved me.

38.

Postcards I mailed to Minneapolis from a motel in Colorado
will not arrive because the boyfriend who saved my life is a fugitive.

39.

I am writing this suicide note because I am l killing the self
that caters to clings to is captured by ex-husbands, ex-therapists,
ex-cons — ex-Catholics!

40.

Do you miss the hugs you will no longer let me give you?
Do you miss the friend you threw away?

41.

What is the price of shame?

42.

The party had started. She was the last to arrive.

Exorcism

"But now, where do I go? The world is men pointing and wringing
their things at you." —Sharon Doubiago

1.
Born silent, silent as the mystery of my mother's womb.
Still waters. Not a wave. Not a ripple.
Neither Mother or I cried. We held our breath, hoping death.

2.
I didn't know how to swim. Mother didn't want to.
Floating would have been a dream. My mother
rode the river well; I cursed and stomped and sank.
Death frequent. Held my mouth closed, my heart open.
Words wriggled between revivals. Those who want
to be saved and born again, *confess*

3.
I rolled on my back and let hymns in. Ah men!

4.
Father was absent at my birth. Did he see me
in his own image and disappear?

Did he see the tangled afterbirth, know he couldn't stop
the Black woman from dying, the baby girls from being born.

There was no one in the room like me.

A small room to be born in.

5.
Father runs through my veins like the money he spent gambling.

6.
Hide and seek. My personality peaks at 35, poetry
separating the white from the riddle and the rhyme.

7.
Father worked nights. Mother was not ripe, or willing. However,
then came Sherry.

8.
I rose to the occasion from my own need to be born.
Save the mother. Drown the father. Love the father.
Hurt the mother. Rise to the occasion.

I can't swim, but I won't drown.

I rose to be pinched and prodded and pushed and pulled
and carved and craved and devoured and spit out, spit at, spewed.
I rose

to fear to hate to touch to eat to kill to curse to seek to cradle
to squash to rely on to bend to break

snakes bigger

than a fist, smaller than a pinky finger

the black girl hidden, the Chinese girl paraded. (The white girl
always the Madonna.) The child born already swaddled.

9.
Yesterday, snake said,

"You need to get some sleep. As to the Madonna-whore dichotomy, it does not
compute with me. Whatever my other shortcomings are, I never divide women
into those categories. All women are sexual—whether they physically do it or not.
It is part of being human. You, on the other hand, evidently have a problem with
that. That dichotomy is inside you, a creation of your mind. Until you deal with
your attitudes, insecurities, and projections, you will be plagued by these types of
feelings and misunderstandings. Continually telescoping interpersonal problems
into societal issues such as misogyny keeps you from dealing with personal
psychological issues. It is a type of avoidance. We have—as all couples do—
interpersonal relationship problems. They need to be dealt with on that level. Stop
making me the stereotypical man and you the stereotypical woman. Start trying to
understand me and how I view the world. It is not what you imagine.
Men and women are different to be sure—and you and I are different from other
men and women. It is a part of our vexation, but it is also part of the joy and
wonder. Vive la difference!"

10.
I sit on a hard chair, hands on keys, drumming

the rhythm constant, consistent until the water breaks
and the penis shrivels.

Mad at Love

Suicide Note Number Three

Dear Johns,

I can't love you: Donkey. Toad. Tyrant. Tempter. Dung.

You can't love me: Goddess, Witch, Whore, Madonna, Love.

A reminder. A commodity. An oddity. A life line. Magnolia blossom.

Mammy. For all your lust and money, I will die.

Unlovable; and yet you loved me. In the dark. Where priests
can't see. I was the guilt, the sin. The desire. The breast. The milk.
The honey. The choke cherry spit

into the light. To be shunned. To be glorified. To be pacified.
To be abused. To be rebuked. To be invisible.

My vulnerability desired, yet despised. I am secret love. I am other.
I am need. I am color. Righteous and ready.

You will die by my heart because love captures the illiterate.
History burns me, spurns me, chattels me. You can't slice
deep enough. The knife slips. Menstrual blood excites you.
My breath, sweet as death.

Silence is your escape.

Don't talk to me. Love me in secret. I will hold your secrets
between my thighs, until I write

All men, so afraid, of not being perfect. I exist to resist
resistance impervious to death

my gravestone is already marked *beloved.*

You who love me can't escape

and will return. Lust is eternal.

Language forever. My words will save me.

I apologize for our lives, for our youth, for our religion.
I apologize to your mothers and my sons.

To die is to grieve is to mourn is to resurrect is to know
there are the ones who will miss me,
who will bring me back.

Love Letter: you should have been there

Dearest,

This is not a *Dear John* letter. This is a love letter. A love letter
to you—or to me—I'm not sure, won't be sure until the writing
is done, until the process has exhausted itself, until the book
has been written and on the shelf.

The process has not always been the same, will not always
be the same. I didn't understand change until the last sentence
presented itself. Future is not found through complacency.

To write is a process, a journey; to live is the same. The process
for one poem, one story, one book is never the same. Change
is the only truth. Process depends on overall character. Depends
on the heart of the book, the blood flowing.

To end a relationship is a process. What worked for the last ending,
won't work for the next one, for this one. Won't work to end
our relationship. Our hearts and blood are sick and thin and tired.
The process of who we are goes back several generations.
We are connected in ways we will never talk about, not connected
in ways we say we are.

Our relationship, like plastic, won't disintegrate. It is possible
to light a match, to set fire, to melt, to liquefy. It is not possible
to write the last chapter. It is not possible to disappear.
This chapter I am writing is the first, another first chapter,
another beginning.

We will gain composure, solidify, contaminate.

I need a new process.

I need to mix glass with stone with sweat. I need to break down,
to sever, to turn to salt, to slice, to mash, to grind, to speak, to sing,
to sway, to leap. I need to set aside stale processes (usable again,
maybe, recycled again, maybe), unworthy of this journey, this cycle,
this new beginning.

I need a new list—no rules—funky aphorisms. I need jasmine
and eucalyptus. I need conversation. I need pizzazz.

I need a photo. A self-portrait of the person I want to become;
the person I already am. I need a photo of me locked in a frame
that breathes, that flows, that fluctuates, yet remains stable.
I will throw away splintered frames with cracked glass.
I can condense, simplify, and adjust to one photo, one me.

You are not in this photo. And, you are not stored in a closet
in a cardboard box. You will never be recycled, again.

You should have been here last winter when I grabbed
a young man on the street who merely said hello. I was hungry
and ate and sipped a glass of fine wine.

You should have been here last spring when my prayers
were answered, hostas in a borrowed garden. Next year
there will be continuity, there will be beauty.

You should have been here last summer when the heat
and humidity rendered me naked on silk sheets,
my sweat sensuous, my bed tossing.

You should have been here this fall when leaves turned
without you, when I traveled to New Orleans and trumpets blared.

This is about lonely; this is about love.

This is about driving to the woods for a fix of your skin,
for conversation, for definition. Desperation.

This is about the five-mile radius you live in; I live far away
with no amenities except diversity, which is oxygen,
not a well with soft water.

This is about painting ceilings, fixing cars, watching movies,
riding bikes, and eating Sushi; about things lost.

About the color purple.

This is about family and dogs and neighbors; about exclusion.

This is about history, about scotch, about coffee, about sex,
about cigarettes; about the future, about nursing homes.

This is about ministers and priests about fantasies and horrors;
about what we despise, what we desire; about velvet trousers,
about heavily starched shirts.

This is about the sting of what I thought I could never have,
the bite of knowing it still doesn't fit; the ache of pretend.

This is about not being mean. It's about metaphor. It's about
getting at truth without spitting. It's about a new way of writing;
a new way of living. It's about story; about understanding story.
It's about kindness. It's about love; about what gets in the way
of love. It's about goodbye. It's about hello. It's about the lost art
of letter writing.

It's about not knowing how to end.

When Do You Leave the Flawed Lover—Or Hold On?

It is the white man lovers who haunt me,
I go to bed with them. They lie right next to my writing table.
I take their stories into my mouth, let out
Jesus Christ, Oh My God, Jesus, Jesus

incorporate their greed
into my I *wanna be loved, baby*

is it the slow release of him that frightens me,
the natural flow, neither of us in danger
of disappearing?

Because he is so easy,
do I return again, and again?

or is it because he's hard? Each thrust

A memory,
     A sign,
          An acknowledgement.

Is it beautiful, this time? Or, just
a needed moment
to remind me?

I awake knowing of a woman.
She is brown.
She is soft.
She loves me.
     I keep my legs crossed, not ready
to give birth to her song
     which is sad, which is honest.

Is it because I won't sing with her
that I can't let her pass?

I am not afraid.
Just haunted by dead birds.
It is not about love, is it? Nor

is it about chance. There's a mystery
here, but I can solve it, if not in this poem,
in another.

There is something about the white
the man
that is familiar,
  ancestral;
that clings to me like the black bird
in the choke cherry tree.

The woman pushes
forward
unplugging a passage;

water will break
when it's ready

> the flood is coming,
> it's coming,
> it's coming . . . .

Hold on.

It's about love

wanting it, needing it, searching for it, embracing it, mis-
interpreting it, shunning it, deceiving it, dying for it, living for it

I want you to know it, to feel it, to recognize it

How do I describe it?
                    It's about death.

How do we embrace death? Can we?

                         an eye for an eye?

It's about love.

Is death genetic?
Does genocide pass from generation to generation?

Can death be forgotten?

    No; *it will always be an ache, a terror, a torment,
    a grieving, a sadness, an insecurity.*

    We will always be angry.

Can we live with death?

    *No, it is not welcome here; we must write, archive death,
    and stop the dying.*

Is writing enough?

    *No; but, writing records, discovers, and challenges. Writing
    lets go of*

Despicable. Derogatory. Disgusting. Desperate.

I love me to death. I write me to life.

> *Love. Loved. Lovely. Love me. Looking for love. Loving.*
> Each form of the word love loosening layers of death.

> *Loosening. Lingering. Lurking.*

Love. I can't leave it alone.

Here you are again, caught

between my throat and my intestines, why
can't I say goodbye

love is so fluffy, so pink, so gracious, so giving, so lovely

so imagined

the diva is vulgar, is dirty, is loud,
is shallow, is shame, is slut

I am mad at love

tongue tickles nipples
arms hug waist
a difficult meditative position
and she topples
below earth, frustrated

I don't want to breathe

there are reasons,
if not
goodbye would be easy

Run Baby Run

These words are not tame,
the grass not tapered, no frill
of a fire line, even sex is wild,
unprotected. No trees pruned,
no saplings purchased. The house
is redeemable

I dream of twelve acres and a dog.
Waiting. For a boy's desire
to press the sheets and dress
the bed.

[It's an old flame. Nothing
hot happens.]

I said no before I came,
so far away from nothing,
but, light rain and a quiet cat
licked me to sleep.
In the depth of night
I tried to run

(usually I'm fast/er)

fear smeared the face I thought
I had grown into like the blue
spruce at full height no longer
blue

but a slut is a slut is a slut
is a the words keep drooling
from the corner of my flat
lips. Fifty-five is just a number,

Baby. When are you going to write
something that matters?

Gazing out the same window?
East or West, hot or cold
        glass shatters
        simultaneously
if you can't drink,
thirst. If you can't love,
close the window.

Fire flies quickly and aphorisms
won't spread your sweet ass,
Baby. One acre or twelve only
one snake holds your mirrors. Go
to the fire with your head hanging
and your ashes will be your mother's
ashes, her tongue tied, her body
boxed and delivered
to a safe space—underground where
the railroad used to be.

All aboard. All aboard.

Avoidance, About Writing

Recently a colleague started cleaning shared office space in a fury. Frantically dusting and polishing and sweeping and moving clutter from one environment to another or trashing it. She admitted she was avoiding yet another challenging job responsibility. Soon everyone in the office was cleaning.

The writing process for me is about avoidance.

I don't write.

I clean my house. I go shopping. I watch a movie. Sex. Sleep.

Eventually the writing will win
no dirt, no money, no libido.

I gather my tools: coffee, cigarettes, potato chips, red licorice, dark chocolate

sit at a dining room table

shuffle papers. I pee. I smoke a cigarette. I drink coffee.

Writing happens when it happens

> *what is it you don't know you know*
> *you must get rid of*

I know I know something, or I wouldn't be sitting here

> *writing is a literary vacuum, it sucks up and eliminates*

I write on recycled paper

slash and surrender: exchange dead words with alive ones

as a first draft simmers I continue to revise
scrutinize the tone, the rhythm—the meaning

draft number two is ready to print
before draft number one has finished printing

each new draft allows me to live vicariously

clutching draft number two I disappear
to smoke a cigarette and read aloud

      if I'm at a house in the woods I read to the Gordon Setter

my creativity exhilarates me

a sassy word, a delicate word,
a word that sings, or a word that singes

tires me

if the man of the house is around, he will stand next to me
listening, smoking; he will touch me, kiss me, distract me

eventually I will toss the writing aside—love making
part of the process

on a good day the process repeats itself
and, again, I've got cleaning and sex on my mind.

A Strong Embrace

Suicide Note Number Four

committing suicide is the most selfish thing a person can do

good
I don't want to make any mistakes

I have tried committing suicide six times (or was it four);
writing saved me.

Was I selfish to think I could end my life?

I was not in control to think at all

like blackouts from historical trauma

all memory lost
mother not divulging her secrets.

Outsiders didn't know I was lonely,
believed I was normal

      a ghost afraid of ghosts haunting myself down.

I am killing Survivor with every story I write

      the more I write, the more I become who I am

I am not selfish.

Only selfish people want Survivor alive
without her they witness their own death.

Recently a student explained that only 15% of us will move
outside the economic class we were born into. How disheartening!
The reason is, she explained, that people stay fixed in the language
of their families. My family spoke in tongues that couldn't be deciphered
by the white folks in our neighborhood. Unfortunately, they couldn't
be deciphered by us, either. My cousin and I agree that we have learned
new language in the academy that allows us to know our experience
as mixed-race, light-skinned black children. How strange is that!?
And, now that we have learned all about oppression from mostly
white women scholars, what do we do with all that learning?

deconstruct it, rip it apart, color it, re-write it,
write suicide notes

Survivor doesn't want to exist

each note a thank you. Thank you,
you've done your job, you've done it well,
good-bye.

My mother said don't tell anyone that you are _____
How could I?
I didn't know I was _____
any more than I knew I was _____

Silence. Invisibility.

It is not selfish to want to be seen,
to be heard

to be beautiful, to be smart, to be proud.

Death a metaphor for life.

Fire in the Bad Girl's Belly

I do not have to give her away. It is the good girl I must kill.

Sometimes I think I know the answer before I ask
the question, before the poem is written/flying from bed
to bed, crushed by night, smothered in starched white
sheets/somewhere love is not waiting, not watching

longing a breath, a breeze, a whimper; tongue gone awry
moth or butterfly

sexy, seductive words surface, and

another poem

I believed in God, it didn't matter, choir boys and ministers
answered prayers; I answered theirs. Mother told me
to stop going to church, took away angels' wings, suggested
kitchen appliances and sterile bedrooms

the woman I was, mourned sainthood. The woman I am
answers my own prayers/refuses temporary accommodations
and unmade beds, accepts fire in the belly of the poem,
fire in the bad girl's belly.

Bold in Her Beauty

I stand next to a beautiful writer
bold in her beauty

It is not an illusion

weeks and months and years of affirmations, of

I am beautiful.

And, she is. And, she always was.

But we never believe it

      linked by a history of *we are not beautiful*

I keep the photograph a secret,
embarrassed by my image, my attitude

insecurity reflected in the moment
the camera has captured the woman I believe I am

I am angry when people say I am beautiful. I know I am not.

      See this photograph and others

ugliness recycled; I am ugly over and over and over again.

My friend is beautiful, is hope

I want the gloom to end here

I have a knife. I cut images of me, slice slowly
reject each negative pronouncement that binds me ugly.

Memory. Metaphor.

A photograph will always be a representation.

It is not real. It is not me. I repeat. It is not real. It is not me.

She wants beautiful. She wants white

it would be expensive and painful

my friend laughs, *consider how you would be different.*

She Has Never Been Afraid

Mother didn't want us to be ugly
so she never told us we were Black,
we were exotic, we were Chinese
even after our Chinese father disappeared,

mostly we were white

I hid in doorways, hid inside the shadows
of my sister who was adventurous, I hid
my tongue and my sex while she twirled
and kissed the captain of the wrestling team

she is kicking me, scratching my face
with razor sharp nails and pulling my fake afro hair

I wrestled with what I didn't know,
writing poems like arms around me
making contact while sister danced

we are always fighting

I stood rigid, away from boys and mother's shame

my sister's baby growing on popcorn,
peanut butter, reefer and acid

I will kill you, Mother said, *and the baby,*

but no one died, and the baby was cute

my first attempt at suicide
death by aspirin

a four hour stay in the emergency room
an underwater ballet

drinking water and waiting, and waiting, and waiting

until the boyfriend who loves me beats me
holds a gun to my head

don't go near the water you might drown

my sister saves me, she has never been afraid
to be beautiful

Mother's arms kept me safe

hid me in her silence, in her sorrow, in her knowing.

Are my arms long enough, strong enough
to hold my sons

who are older now than I was when they were born?

Are they struggling to escape the canal of their mother's
damned self, struggling to escape the addictions
that have kept them safe

safety an oxymoron, purgatory a holding cell for hope
not to die before we know why death is necessary,

why mothers are not angry enough, why sons can't love
their mothers and mothers can't love their daughters,
an angel told me

my mother would never love me the way I needed her,
I listened. How could she love me, my face her mirrored
image—did I remind her of her childhood, her teenage years,
her marriage to a man she wouldn't let love her because
the pot was black and boiling/

if I failed, Mother would fail again and again reliving
the ugliness of slavery, the Ku Klux Klan, lynching,
rape, race riots, neighbors with guns

not passing was never a choice

better to hate the daughter, hate her with all the protection
protection provides; give her a cold, closed box
to numb her from expectations or desires

we can't be hurt if we stay silent and invisible—can we?

Hate happened before my sons were born, before
I was born, before my mother was born;
the memory marks us.

It's okay to be angry, but not at my mother—I hope

Mother was angry, I hope in death she found her way
to finally embrace anger, shed her white safety net

darkness must come before the light, I write

this note for my sons, to relieve them of Grandmother's fears
her voice heard only once-in-awhile as soap in my mouth
or a broken yard stick. To relieve them of their mother's anger
swift movements of men of homes of jobs

Who has maimed my mother, and me?

If it wasn't you, I apologize, but until I no longer write, anger
holds me
                    I am not a righteous, racist, sexist, bigot, I am not

willing to live your lies, I am not willing

to be shamed

                    I am not a righteous, racist, sexist, bigot, I am not

I love my sons, how has my madness hurt them?
Do they know I am healing? Can they believe addiction
is not a disease, but a craving for wealth?

I can't change history. How many of us don't know
what is killing us?

We think it is our fault. We believe we are bad. We believe
we are ugly. We believe we are worthless. We believe
we can have the American Dream

Mother knew we can't, but prayed, prayed often, prayed silently

I know we can't, but pray, pray reactively, pray loudly,
pray myself to death/to life each suicide note a prayer.

Sane Asylum Café in the Woods

Ambivalence carried me twenty-five miles from the city
to the woods

a place I didn't want to be
      blank pages, words flying
I had nowhere else to go
      concentrate on the writing. I was hungry.

      Nikki Giovanni said *to write about meatloaf*

      I lost the recipe.
      I am not hungry for poems.
      Maybe tomorrow, I will mix loneliness and longing

            Heat oven to 325
            Bake 45 minutes

      smell the Black mother, the missing Chinese father;

      taste forgiveness.

      No one has rescued me; in the woods, I know how it feels
to sit and wait.

      I felt awkward, in the city, about being older and not hip
in the way the young Asian women were hip. Who was I
to party with them?

      I was late for dinner.

      [At the same time I was thinking—if any derelict on the street
stopped me and said come live with me/marry me, I would.]

I was tired and needed a hug.

Midnight, this night, blue spruce and pines welcomed me.
Blair, the Gordon Setter, welcomed me, bone in mouth.

Two lit candles on the dining room table, two glasses
of red wine, and two salads.

He remembers when we were nineteen and made love
his first time

forty years later my need is conditional.

I want only moments.

The salad was perfect: romaine, green olives, walnuts,
carrots, parmesan cheese and vinaigrette dressing.

We fell asleep clinging to ourselves.

Writing on a Good Day

Sometimes I write *notes* when I'm feeling happy,
on a good day at a cabin in the woods, away

> from the city where my heart beats irregularly
> snagged by the tedious rhythms of lonely.

In the woods, my lover comes from planting evergreens
slow like hot sun seeping into madness,
winter skin released

> *what will I wear to work on Monday should I rent a video*
> *my friend is having surgery in two days I will be teaching*
> *in six days AA the price of gas is $2.25 my gas tank*
> *is empty the silk camisole I bought at the Goodwill*
> *is hand washable the polka dot sun dress I bought*
> *from the Salvation Army doesn't fit the $1.99 Royal*
> *Dutton Kirkwood Platter from the Goodwill is worth*
> *$69.95 I hope we have pork chops for dinner tonight*

I am

as relaxed as I get amidst
twelve acres of dirt, twigs, saplings, and giant trees

I don't have to do any thing.
I don't want to go any place.
I don't need to run or hide.

An unusual time to write
when anger, anxiety, and recklessness sleep.

Sunlight disappears, shadows a dog napping,
a pen displays *Delano Chevrolet-Oldsmobile*
I eat tortilla chips.

I don't know where my lover is; it doesn't matter.
He's on a tractor or sawing branches.
He's sleeping or he's smoking.
I release him as easily as he releases me.
We're lovers and we're friends.
On good days, this works.

My angel, my ghosts, my Aunt Grace are quiet.
What is my process of writing?

I fit into process like my clothes which I change frequently
or like today, I am naked, nothing to hide no one to be.

I write odes to blackbirds and great horned owls
to evergreens and blue spruce

the lover will ask to hear what the woman has written
applauds, if it's about a man and a dog in the woods.

I Want to Live

Suicide Note Number Five

Experience is synonymous with identity.

I started writing poetry to visualize the Black Chinese woman that I and no one else could see. My vocabulary was limited, my sentences were blunt like a cheap knife. Words sawed across white fences disrupting quiet neighborhoods. I had no love to embrace, and no love was embracing me. Mixed-marriages disappeared on roads under construction.

I clung to my poems even though they were ragged. They were edgy, zigzagging their way into black holes. I owned them. I collected them. I honored them. I wrote more poems. I escaped gated neighborhoods and small minded, fearful neighbors that lived there—including me.

I entered communities where my poems could live, where metaphor banished the girl and bridled the woman. Where I learned that commas and semi-colons slowed the narrative, periods meant stop, breathe. Where no punctuation meant the poem is raving, ravenous, relentless, out of control.

Stamina: The problem with entering new communities is sometimes the community has too many rules. Rules that may not consider all of us.

Stamina: Sometimes we believe that academic communities should embrace us because only diversity can make academic communities smarter. Most of the time we embrace the academy because we think the academy can make us smarter (richer).

Stamina: So we give everything we are to the Community, while the Community uses, abuses, ignores, or patronizes us.

Eventually, we earn our degrees, but learn from the gossip of gurus
that we can't write. So we don't write. We stop writing.

Yet, we are writers. Familiarity embraces us on the outskirts
of literary streets. We find the women and the men that look like us.
The writers who speak in tongues whose poems are brave.
Many have side-stepped the academy, but they know craft and
are crafty—creating a vernacular that is ours. No one can dismiss
the accuracy and loveliness of our sharp-witted words.

Because we have faith we begin to write again.

I don't write every day, at a particular time or in a particular place.
I write wherever, whenever a particular muse insists that I write.

Sometimes, I write when I can't find any excuse not to write.

Sometimes, I don't write because I am lazy.

Sometimes, I don't write because most of my energy
goes to pursuing and maintaining relationships (stamina
a curse I can't release).

No, this is a lie.

Writing is more than an act of putting pen to paper or fingers
on a key board. The real part of writing is the gut wrenching,
heart breaking, oppressive experiences witnessed and lived
that a writer must write about.

When I write, I must keep myself safe.

I capture my hot heart in memory. Identity unmasked. Abstract
words become mantra. I chant *I am beautiful, I am brilliant, I am loved,*

until I become story. I let me into the world. Give myself visibility.
Sometimes I dance. Sometimes I sing. Sometimes I need a friend,
a lover, or a therapist.

Sometimes I must keep my distance and can only name myself *she*.

It is scary to be vulnerable and risqué. Death nudges me along like
a woman ready to save her life.

My mother died of a leukemia blast. Her body was covered with
black and blue bruises. The bruises intensified the closer she was
to love.

Haunted by Mother's bruises, I turned them into metaphor, larger
than my mother, larger than me. They became answers to questions
I had stopped asking.

When I said goodbye to stamina both the woman and the writer
were free and capable of love—writing it, giving it, receiving it.

Stamina another word for control.

I Didn't Know I Wasn't Breathing

For forty years my boots tried to fit
the stirrups of prancing white horses.

Giddy-up! Giddy-up!

I clutched leather reins, refused to fall off. Momentum
and no slowing down. Around and around and around.

I wore anxiety like a clock with no alarm. Years ticked away
I didn't know I wasn't breathing.

There was no revolution.

There was only kicking the horse, and kicking the horse,
and kicking the horse.

The horse was nailed down.

> *When did I wake up, tired of revolving in slow moving circles?*

I've been young for too many years. Today the saddle comes off.
It is the beginning of winter. No more ponies.

Youth was a time of too much. Old age has its own needs.

Gravity is the anxiety I felt when I woke this morning.

> *Dear Youth, it's over.*

This morning I woke up tired of kicking.

This morning I woke up.

Poem After Poem After Poem: I write a book

My orange Vega is a beacon on a snowy night.
I slide and spin on icy roads to the college built
in the midst of potato farms. I am far away from South Minneapolis.
But I will return home in my writing.

I sit in the back of my *Women in Literature* class so no one
will notice me, no one will ask me to speak.

I hear whispers, "she's a lesbian." And, "why is there a man
in this class?"

By break, the man is gone.

I am not a bra burner, but a born again Christian.

We read *The Wanderground*, and are told to wander
through any bookstore; I find

there are no books about me!
Nothing about a Black/Chinese woman

in the feminist bookstore,
nothing about a Black/Chinese woman passing for White!

Sunday, I skip Prayer and Praise, stay home to rant and rave
sketching myself on paper, poem after poem after poem

a portrait of me.

Shots of Johnny Walker Red keep me sober until graduation,
escape is easy. I stop singing in the choir. I write a book.

Words sing on the page.

Now, I am a woman in literature.

At Some Point Your Notes Begin to Make Sense

Suicide notes are living, breathing, speaking.
Listen. Love them. Forgive them.

Share them. Someone is listening. And there are others.

We all want to say our goodbyes and live our life.

Writing our life can be easy—there are angels; reading our life
can be hard

     1. work with a therapist
     2. work with a writing mentor

I read and re-live and re-read and re-live my notes until I'm done
and I know

I can handle revision.

Notes multiply. Name them. Connect them. Bind them.

Risk an ending

be careful what you give away—family, friends, home
later, you might want them back

risk a new beginning.

At some point your notes begin to make sense. They no longer hurt
or haunt you. They save you. Awareness is a safety issue,
a health issue

see patterns, texture, complexity, and color

there are many reasons for a *no*. *Yes,* happens.

It's True What They Say, I Am a Writer

Yes, I have a writer's curriculum vitae ten pages long.
Each line item is a step in a tumultuous journey of survival.
I write to survive.
I started in second grade.
I should have started in kindergarten.
I should have started before the day I was born.

I remember what I need to remember.
The rest of it I make up or avoid.
Imagination is the same as truth.

I am not as bad as I imagine.
I am good.
There is no good or bad there is only better.

Every word, every phrase, every verse I write
is a blessed breath, a will to live,
a protest against invisibility,
a protest against death.

I am a writer.

I teach writing.
Yes, writing can be taught.
I can teach you.
I can teach you to create a curriculum vitae.
Each line item a blessed step in your life's journey.

Writing can save your life.

The first photo taken of me was in front of our stucco house
on a hill in South Scandinavian Minneapolis. I am dressed
in blue silk Chinese pajamas with tiny pink frog closures.

The mandarin collar is choking my smile.

I am looking away from the camera.
Down the street.
Past the Lutheran church.
Past the houses of little blonde girls who attend
the Lutheran church Sunday school with me.

Past the family I don't know.
The family that does not recognize me.

The family that dignifies me by binding my feet
         in black brocade Chinese slippers.
The family that poses me in front of the dolly buggy
         where the blue-eyed baby-doll is comforted
         by my brown-arm embrace.
Caretaking, for me, comes from a history of caretaking.
It's hard to shake. Mama shook it, though.

Mama shook her Black mama, her Black siblings.
She shook her Black grandma and the plantation owner's son
who claimed he loved her. Great-grandma said no and meant it.
But, she accepted the gift of a pig.

(We do what we have to, to survive.)

My mama's family had dignity. Integrity. Didn't matter, though.
Babies were still born.
Women were raped.

Mama shook the south and southerners and Black Baptists.

She shook so hard, like Black Sambo who gave away

his purple shoes and hat. My sisters and I were the yellow,
creamy butter she got in return for all of her sacrifices.

All her shaking, however, didn't make my mother thin.
She was fat in lies and deception.

She was fat from carrying five babies, fat from sheltering,
and protecting those babies into adulthood. She taught us
to fit in, to blend, to hide, to be invisible. She also taught us,
if the neighbors and the school children didn't believe we were
White—be Chinese. Be exotic. Wear embroidered silk,
play mah jong, eat chow mein.

Mother fantasized about Chinese men.
She read romance novels about British ladies and Asian men.
She loved my Chinese father.

We could be Chinese, she said, but only when we couldn't be White;
we could never be Black.

Mama shook so hard. She shook so hard Daddy disappeared.
I was five years old.
The only history I don't have to imagine is a five year old girl
in Chinese pajamas in front of a doll buggy in front of cement steps,
in front of a stucco house on a hill in an all white neighborhood.

I seductively paraded my baby Asian exoticism
at the Powderhorn Park doll buggy parade

(sadness can easily be mistaken for seduction).

This is the first line on my curriculum vitae: 1953,
I am five years old, my daddy has disappeared.

What is the first line on your curriculum vitae?

On a day when you are sad, when you are lonely,
when you don't love yourself, get a notebook, a reliable pen.
Write a book. A memoir, or maybe you'll call it fiction.

Take your time, don't rush.
        What is it you remember?
        What is it you imagine?
        Name the chapters.
        What is your theme?
        What carries your journey as a hero forward,
                and back, and forward?
Give your book a title.

Then, put your notes away.
Wait a day or two or a week or a month.
Wait until the next time you're feeling sad, you're feeling lonely,
you're feeling worthless, you're feeling you have no purpose in life.
Then, begin, again.

Not necessarily at the beginning, the chronology will sort itself
when it needs sorting. Begin with what's on your mind now!
What obsesses you? Who are you mad at, in love with, jealous of?

I am Chinese and Black, but grew up passing for White.
My theme is overcoming invisibility and silence.

Your theme will slowly become visible as you write,
the more you write.
When you discover it, name it.
Say it aloud.
Remember it.
Imagine it.

Write towards it.

My story is sewn together with words on paper bags, *Post-it* notes,
and recycled paper; words published and unpublished.
Words read to small audiences and to no one but myself.
Words that save me.

You and I will keep writing. We will know what love is
and we will give it away.

That's Where She is Now

In the back of his house there are blue
trees, thirty feet tall, thick
like history. The spruce
cast shadows aqua blue,
baby green. Seeped in mystery.
Each tree a pyramid. Sunlight
slinking around another
untrimmed day. A trillion
angels' wings almost touch
dense ground, hang down, test
space. The stamina of miracles.
Each needle rests on protective
limbs. Trust measured
in increments of relationships.
The tops of blue spruce are almost
there. That's where she is
now. Between sky and earth.
Surrounded by Scotch, Norway,
Austrian: white pines. Somewhere
at the top, spider webs stop, are
neither intricate nor beautiful.
Beauty is white lace, only
if she is a woman wanting,
or snowflakes on the tongue
if she hasn't already tasted metal.
Sometimes a butterfly hovers near
and she feels freedom.
But, is it what we imagine?
Love mocks tenacity as well
as flight. Love. Feverish fools
have the answer. Love. Every
inch of every thirty foot blue tree.
Love. Angels' hair laced
with black spiders.

And, Finally, There is Quiet

It's insane, this tranquility,
it's insane, and
I adore it. When did I claim
the ocean was my muse?
Was I so large, so loud
I didn't notice. Whisper.
Invite me back to hear
the melody of fallen
water. To cross
the narrow bridge
where time has frozen/
imagine snow topped pines
so tall they exhale heaven!
What worried me was life
when life was not the question.
Nothing happens; time waits
until I'm ready. There are
no stars, there are only secrets.
Tonight, for once, I have none
to tell. Finally, there is quiet.

Notes

Death Wears Black

"When artists render up the truth of their lives and those of others, it is as if they are cartographers introducing us to foreign worlds. Even with that, the world of pain is a place unreadable by many. Sometimes it is the pain of the earth, not of any one individual."

> —Linda Hogan, from *The Woman Who Watches Over the World*, W.W. Norton & Company, 2001, page 195

Exorcism

"But now, where do I go? The world is men pointing and wringing their things at you."

> —Sharon Doubiago, from *My Father's Love*, forthcoming

About the Author

SHERRY QUAN LEE, author of *Chinese Blackbird* (an underground favorite), Asian American Renaissance, 2002, approaches writing as a community resource and as culturally based art of an ordinary everyday practical aesthetic. She is a Distinguished Alumni of North Hennepin Community College. Currently, she is the Program Associate for the Split Rock Arts Program summer workshops and the Online Mentoring for Writers Program at the University of Minnesota where she also earned her MFA in Creative Writing.

Recently retired from ten years of teaching Creative Writing at Metropolitan State University, Saint Paul, Minnesota, Quan Lee facilitates community workshops at Intermedia Arts (SASE: The Write Place Literary Programs), and elsewhere. She was a first year, 1996, participant of Cave Canem, a writing retreat for Black poets.

You can learn more about Sherry Quan Lee and view more of her work at www.SherryQuanLee.com.

About the Artist

KURT SEABERG is an artist and illustrator living in Minneapolis, Minnesota. Born in Chicago in 1954, he studied art, literature and creative writing at the University of Washington, graduating with a Bachelor of Arts degree in 1976. He continued his studies at the University of Minnesota in the 1980s, where he learned intaglio and lithography. Since then, he has exhibited his prints and published his illustrations widely for many years. The cover of this book features his 1992 lithograph *Temple Guardians*.

"One of the tasks of the artist," he says, "is to remind us where our strength and power lies—in beauty, community and a sense of place. Nature has always been a theme and source of inspiration in my work, in particular the spiritual qualities that I find there. My hope is that my art will evoke the same feelings that arise in me when I contemplate the mystery of being alive in a living world: humility, gratitude and a sense of wonder before what I believe is truly sacred."

You can learn more about Seaberg and view more of his work at www.KurtSeaberg.com.

Printed in the United States
203743BV00001B/23-72/P

Contents

Getting Started